Of the Fields, Lately

DAVID FRENCH

David French's *Of the Fields, Lately* won the Chalmer's Drama Award for Outstanding New Play of 1973. Since then it has received countless productions, including a trip to Broadway. Mr. French has also won awards for his other plays in the Mercer series: *Leaving Home, Salt-Water Moon, 1949*, as well as the comedy, *Jitters*. He was born in Newfoundland and now divides his time between Toronto and the Maritimes.

*

Of the Fields, Lately was first performed at the Tarragon Theatre, Toronto, September 29, 1973, and directed by Bill Glassco, with the following cast:

BEN MERCER	*Tim Henry*
JACOB MERCER	*Sean Sullivan*
MARY MERCER	*Florence Paterson*
WIFF ROACH	*Sandy Webster*

Of the Fields, Lately

David French

ANANSI

First published in 1975 by New Press.
Published in 1981 by General Paperbacks.
Published in 1985 by Stoddart Publishing.
Published in 1991 by House of Anansi Press Ltd.

This edition published in 2007 by
House of Anansi Press Inc.
110 Spadina Avenue, Suite 801
Toronto, ON, M5V 2K4
Tel. 416-363-4343 • Fax 416-363-1017
www.anansi.ca

Distributed in Canada by
HarperCollins Canada Ltd.
1995 Markham Road
Scarborough, ON, M1B 5M8
Toll free tel. 1-800-387-0117

Distributed in the United States by
Publishers Group West
1700 Fourth Street
Berkeley, CA 94710
Toll free tel. 1-800-788-3123

House of Anansi Press is committed to protecting our natural environment. As part
of our efforts, this book is printed on Rolland Enviro paper: it contains 100%
post-consumer recycled fibres, is acid-free, and is processed chlorine-free.

Rights to produce *Of the Fields, Lately* in whole or in part,
in any medium by any group, amateur or professional, are retained by the author.
Interested persons are requested to apply for permission to Charles Northcote,
Core Literary Inc., 140 Wolfrey Ave., Toronto ON, M4K 1L3, 416-466-4929
charlesnorthcote@rogers.com.

11 10 09 08 07   4 5 6 7 8

LIBRARY AND ARCHIVES CANADA CATALOGUING IN PUBLICATION DATA

French, David, 1939–
Of the fields, lately

A play.
ISBN-13: 978-0-88784-508-6
ISBN-10: 0-88784-508-8

I. Title.

PS8561.R45045   1991   C812'.54   C91-093642-0
PR9199.3.F7404   1991

The photographs in this book are by Robert Barnett and Charles Lapp.

Canada Council   Conseil des Arts
for the Arts   du Canada

ONTARIO ARTS COUNCIL
CONSEIL DES ARTS DE L'ONTARIO

*We acknowledge for their financial support of our publishing program
the Canada Council for the Arts, the Ontario Arts Council, and the Government of Canada
through the Book Publishing Industry Development Program (BPIDP).*

Printed and bound in Canada

For all fathers and sons

As for man, his days are as grass: as a flower of the field, so he flourisheth. For the wind passeth over it and it is gone; and the place thereof shall know it no more.

Psalm 103, 15-16

The scene: A house in Toronto, January, 1961.

ACT I
Scene 1 — early Sunday evening:
Scene 2 — two hours later.

ACT II
Scene 1 — Monday morning:
Scene 2 — early Monday evening

ACT ONE

Scene One

Limbo. Light up on BEN.

BEN

(to the audience) It takes many incidents to build a wall between two men, brick by brick. Sometimes you're not aware of the building of the wall, and sometimes you are, though not always strong enough or willing enough to kick it down. It starts very early, as it did with my father and me, very early. And it becomes a pattern that is hard to break until the wall is made of sound brick and mortar, as strong as any my father ever built. Time would not level it. Only death.

I don't know if my father ever remembered one such incident. He never spoke of it to me, but I often thought it was the emotional corner-stone of the wall between us.

Light up on JACOB.

JACOB

It was summer, 1952, and I had just come home from work, later than usual. It was going on nine in the evening, and as I stepped in the door, Mary said to me, "Ain't tonight the night Ben's team plays for the championship?"

BEN

He rushed out the door and down to the school-yard, the first game he had ever come to, and my mother put his supper in the oven, for later ... I hadn't reminded my father of the game. I was afraid he'd show up and embarrass me. Twelve years old, and ashamed of my old man. Ashamed of his dialect, his dirty overalls, his bruised fingers with the fingernails lined with dirt, his teeth yellow as old ivory. Most of all, his lunchpail, that symbol of the working man. No, I wanted a doctor for a father. A lawyer. At least a fireman. Not a carpenter. That wasn't good enough . . . And at home my mother sat down to darn his socks and watch the oven . . . I remember stepping up to bat. The game was tied; it was the last of the ninth, with no one on base. Then I saw him sitting on the bench along third base. He grinned and waved, and gestured to the man beside him.

JACOB *(at game)*
That's my son.

BEN
But I pretended not to see him. I turned to face the pitcher. And angry at myself, I swung hard on the first pitch, there was a hollow crack, and the ball shot low over the short-stop's head for a double. Our next batter bunted and I made third. He was only a few feet away now, my father.

JACOB
Ben! Ben! Over here! Ben!

BEN
But I still refused to acknowledge him. Instead, I stared hard at the catcher, pretending concentration. And when the next pitch bounced between the catcher's legs and into home screen, I slid home to win the game.

JACOB
His team-mates pounced on him and hefted him up on their shoulders and lugged him around the infield. A hero.

BEN
And there he was, jumping up and down, showing his teeth, excited as hell.

JACOB
'Ben!' I shouted my level best. 'Ben!' And I seen him look my way . . . and then look off . . . *(Light fades slowly on JACOB.)*

BEN

And as the crowd broke up and our team stampeded out of the school-yard, cleats clicking and scraping blue sparks on the sidewalk, I looked back once through the wire fence and saw my father still sitting on the now-empty bench, alone, slumped over a little, staring at the cinders between his feet, just staring ... I don't know how long he stayed there, maybe till dark, but I do know he never again came down to see me play. At home that night he never mentioned the game or being there. He just went to bed unusually early ...

A hymn begins: "Abide with Me", softly at first as BEN turns and walks into the kitchen, removes his shirt and drops it into the bushel basket beside the ironing board. The light has been slowly fading, and the hymn rising in volume as the light fades to black, then comes up onstage.

The stage is divided into two rooms: living-room and kitchen. In addition there is a hallway with the front door offstage. A staircase leads up from the hallway to the second floor, to the bedrooms and bathroom, all unseen.

The kitchen contains an ironing board, a small arborite table and four chairs, a stove, fridge, cupboards over the sink containing dishes, a wall telephone, a calendar and kitchen prayer. There is also a back door leading off the kitchen and a window.

The living-room contains a bay window, a knick-knack cabinet, chesterfield and arm-chair, T.V. and radio. There are various family photographs around the room.

It is a few minutes past seven, Sunday evening, January, 1961.

JACOB sits on the chesterfield in the living-room, listening with a preoccupied look to the hymn which comes from a nearby radio. He wears casual clothes.

MARY is in the kitchen, ironing. She sings along with the hymn. There is a bushel basket of clothing on the floor beside the ironing board, and now and then she helps herself to a shirt or blouse, irons and folds it. She wears black.

MARY

Remember that time Dot and me was crossing Water Street with Ben in the carriage? You and Wiff was behind.

JACOB looks up and turns down the radio.

The streetcar had stopped to let us cross, and that old car shot out from behind it and took the carriage right out of our hands.

JACOB
Can still hear the t'ump. And you screaming like a tea-kettle.

MARY
Poor Dot. She fainted dead away. T'ought he was killed for sure. Remember that?

JACOB
A wonder he wasn't, the way the carriage was all squashed up.

MARY
A miracle she called it. Suppose it was . . . *(pause)*

JACOB
He hardly said hello, Mary . . .

MARY
What?

JACOB
Two years away, and he hardly gives me a glance.

MARY
Well, give him time, he just got in. Besides, you wasn't much better, the way you kept your distance.

JACOB
Not so much as a handshake . . .

MARY
Perhaps if you'd put your hand out first . . .

JACOB
Yes, and have him chop it off. *(He rises, crosses to archway.)* What's he home for? Did he say?

MARY

Dot's funeral, I imagine.

JACOB

What? All the ways from Saskatchewan? He wasn't that close to Dot.

MARY

Look, Jake, I don't know any more than you do. I was just as surprised as you when he walked in just now. He never mentioned he was coming home.

JACOB

You sure, Mary?

MARY

Well, you was listening into my ear when I called him yesterday. Did I once ask him to? Did I?

At that moment BEN comes down the stairs, and JACOB returns to the chesterfield. BEN's hair is slightly long, and he wears blue jeans and a white T-shirt. He looks at JACOB, who looks away and turns up the radio. BEN enters the kitchen.

BEN

My shirt ready yet, Mom?

MARY

Not yet, my son. Did you find everyt'ing okay?

BEN

Yeah. Hey, I like the new house.

MARY

Do you?

Ben goes to the fridge and pours himself a glass of milk and takes a biscuit from the bread-box.

BEN
You surprised to see me, Mom?

MARY
I still ain't recovered.

BEN
You don't seem too excited.

MARY
Don't I?

BEN
No. I thought you would be.

MARY
Well, you never said you was coming home when I talked to you on the phone. You never gave any hint.

BEN
So what? I'm impulsive, okay?

MARY
I only called to let you know about Aunt Dot. I never expected you to come all this ways. Why did you?

BEN
How's Uncle Wiff taking it?

MARY
Wiff? Don't mention Wiff to me.

BEN
You two still not getting along?

MARY
I never expected him to sink as low as he done this time.

BEN
Why? What'd he do now?

MARY

Never had the decency to go down to the hospital when Dot died. His own wife.

BEN

Really?

MARY

Not a word of a lie. The hospital phoned to tell him Dot never had long, so he called us. Then he never showed up. Later, we drove up to the Oakwood and found him drunk at one of the tables. Couldn't stand on his own. *(slight pause)* Ben?

BEN

What?

MARY

You never answered my question. Why did you come home?

BEN

Why? I wanted to. What do you mean why? I liked Aunt Dot. Do I have to have any other reason? *(MARY just looks at him.)* All right. I wanted to see you, too. Is that good enough? Missed your cooking. *(He hugs her.)* Hey, you lost weight.

MARY

What about your father?

BEN

What about him?

MARY

Don't he enter into it? He lives here, too. He ain't just a stick of furniture, you know.

BEN

Look, if you don't want me here, Mom, just say so . . .

MARY

At least you could speak to him. Is that too much to ask? A few words, at least.

BEN

I already said hello. What more do you want? He doesn't want to talk to me.

MARY

Don't he? *(slight pause)* You might've shook his hand, Ben. He stood there, waiting . . . Both of you too proud to make the first move. What a pair.

BEN

How come he's listening to the church service? He never used to.

MARY

That's not'ing. He even lets me drag him there on occasion—Christmas and Easter.

BEN

What's happened to him?

MARY

Who knows, my son? Never t'ought I'd see that day, though, did you? *(slight pause)* Ben?

BEN

Yeah?

MARY

I'm telling you right now, there's to be no fighting. Is that understood? I won't have it.

BEN

Don't worry. I won't start anything.

MARY

No, and don't finish it, either, or else. *(BEN looks at her.)* Or *else.*

BEN

What if he picks on me? What then? What am I supposed to do, let him?

MARY
Ignore him.

BEN
Just like that?

MARY
Yes, just like that. He ain't a well man, Ben, and I don't want him upset.

BEN
Why? What's wrong with him? His back still bothering him?

MARY
What? . . .

BEN
His back.

MARY
Oh, yes . . .

BEN
What does the doctor say? Is he okay now?

MARY
Look, why don't you go in and speak to him. Break the ice. Go on now. And don't forget what I said. No fighting.

BEN enters the living-room, takes a few hesitant steps towards his father, stops, his hands jammed into his pockets. He is about to return to the kitchen when JACOB turns his head.

JACOB
(*quickly*) How was your flight?

This stops BEN.

BEN
(*turns*) What? . . .

JACOB
The plane ride . . . You never said . . . How was it?

He switches off the radio. During this scene they look awkwardly at one another, separated by a continent of a few feet. Each waits for the other to speak first and each suffers the discomfort of self-consciousness.

BEN
Oh? . . . Bumpy . . . You know.

MARY
You used to like those old planes, Jake. He was up a lot during the War. Wasn't you, boy?

BEN
(to JACOB) Yeah?

JACOB
(to BEN) When I worked at the Gander . . . I was there when Dr. Banting crashed. We heard his plane take off that morning in the fog, and not long afterwards we heard he went down . . .

Pause.

BEN
(finally, for something to say) Didn't Uncle Fred work for the Air Force or something? Around the same time?

JACOB
No, the Army.

BEN
Was it the Army? *(He nods.)*

MARY
Tell him about Fred, Jake. How he couldn't read or write, and he was putting up towers.

JACOB
No, he don't want to hear about that. A telegram would arrive from Ottawa, and Fred'd say to the nearest man, "Read it, I left my glasses home." What a man. Couldn't read or write his own name, and he was building towers for the Army. *(pause)* Don't let on I said it, but your mother was worried half to death, these past two years.

MARY
Who was? I heard that.

BEN
What for? I can take care of myself.

JACOB
Well, you might've wrote more often. Four or five letters ain't much. There was months there we never knowed whether you'd been kidnapped or killed.

BEN
It's not the Wild West any more, you know.

JACOB
That ain't the p'int, now, and you knows it. Don't argue.

MARY
Jake!

BEN
Dad, look . . .

JACOB
What's you doing out there? Is you still working?

BEN
Yeah. Didn't Mom tell you?

JACOB
Don't tell me you'm still sorting letters at the Post Office?

BEN

So? What's wrong with that?

JACOB

Ah, my Jesus . . .

BEN

It's a job, okay? I don't know what I want to do yet.

JACOB

That's for men without schooling. You went to university.

BEN

Yeah, for two whole months. Big deal.

JACOB

Whose fault is that? Mine, I suppose?

BEN

Did I say it was anybody's fault? Did I?

JACOB

No, and that you didn't. Well, don't blame me. You didn't
have to run off and quit school, just because I struck you once.

BEN

Once?

JACOB

How many times did my own father take the skin off me, and
I never held a grudge. I never let it ruin my life, a few strokes
of the belt.

MARY

All right, that's enough! Ben, get in here quick and get your
shirt.

BEN

(to JACOB) I didn't come home to fight, okay? I came for the

funeral. So lay off. *(He enters the kitchen.)*

JACOB
Would you've come home so quick if *I*'d died?

MARY
What a t'ing to say, Jake. Shame on you.

JACOB
(to himself, as he switches on the radio) Be lucky if he sent
flowers . . .

Another hymn plays.

MARY
(angrily) I t'ought I asked you not to fight with him? Not home
ten minutes and already it's started. If there's any more of
that, you can go straight back where you came from, and I
means it. I won't warn you again.

BEN
Look, you asked me to talk to him, Mom. It was your idea.

MARY
Talk, yes.

BEN
So I tried.

MARY
Did you?

BEN
Yeah, I did.

JACOB
What's you two doing in there, Mary—scheming?

MARY
No, we're not scheming. *(to BEN)* He don't hear too well these

14

days, except when he ain't supposed to.

JACOB
Instead of plotting behind my back, you'd best get ready. Wiff'll soon be here and he's still half-naked.

MARY
Well, *I*'m ready. Is you? I don't see you getting dressed in a hurry.

JACOB
No, I'll wrinkle my good suit if I sits around. *(then)* T'row me out yesterday's paper. I ain't finished it yet.

MARY
(winking at BEN) What's wrong with your two feet, boy?

JACOB
Not'ing. I just don't wish to *intrude,* Mary. *(He turns up the radio.)*

BEN
See? That's what I mean, Mom. That.

MARY
Never mind. Get dressed and forget it. Pretend you don't hear. That's what I does.

BEN crosses to the foot of the stairs, buttoning his shirt.

JACOB
And change your pants. You'm not wearing old blue jeans down to the funeral parlour.

BEN
Did I say I was?

MARY
Leave him alone, Jake!

JACOB

Uncle Wiff'll want you for a pallbearer on Tuesday, now you'm home.

MARY

Your dark suit's still in our closet, my son. I kept it. Didn't need to be cleaned or pressed, even.

JACOB

Well, shine your shoes. Have some respect for your Aunt Dot, if you got none for yourself. *(BEN goes up the stairs.)* And cut your hair!

With that JACOB switches off the radio and rises with sudden weariness. He wanders into the kitchen, looks for the newspaper on top of the fridge.

MARY

A fine welcome home this is. And you wonders why he stays away?

JACOB

Oh, he'll be back, Mary, as long as you'm alive. No fear of that, my lady. He ain't home to see me. That much is certain.

MARY

Can't you just be civil, Jake?

JACOB

Civil?

MARY

Yes, you've heard of the word. He's only home for two days.

JACOB

T'ank God.

MARY

Yes, you'll be some glad to see him go, won't you? Then you can go back to reading his letters on the sly.

JACOB

Never even asked how I was . . . T'inks more of his Aunt Dot than he do of me.

MARY

That ain't true.

JACOB

Even when I was in the hospital, did I get so much as a Get Well card? Poor Billy was there every weekend. If it'd been you, Mary . . .

MARY

Keep your voice down . . .

JACOB

And you expects me to be civil? Well, he can kiss my ass, and you can tell him so for me. Is that civil enough?

MARY

Look, Jake, don't let's quarrel on account of Ben, okay? We've been fine, ain't we, just the two of us, until now? Ain't we?

JACOB

Not a harsh word between us. *(He sits at the table with his newspaper.)*

MARY

So let's keep it that way. We was never so close as when the boys left, never. *(slight pause)* Why, I even went to wrestling.

JACOB

And who went to bingo with you and Dot once a week, rain or shine?

MARY

Well, don't spoil it then. Don't let him be a wedge between us. Not again. *(then)* Go on, boy. Read your newspaper. Find somet'ing in there to complain about. *(pause)* I don't t'ink I'll go to bingo anymore, Jake.

JACOB

Oh? Just when I was getting the hang of it.

MARY

No. My heart ain't in it anymore, boy. Won't seem the same without Dot . . . *(Her attention is suddenly focussed on JACOB, who holds the newspaper close, then studies it at arm's length.)* "The wise man's eyes are in his head; but the fool walketh in darkness."

JACOB

What?

MARY

Ecclesiastes.

JACOB

And wha'ts that supposed to mean, may I ask? "The fool walketh in darkness."

MARY

That's where you'll be, my son, in darkness, if you don't soon get glasses.

JACOB

Ah . . . *(He rises and gets MARY's glasses from a cupboard shelf. A pair with rhinestones and winged sides.)*

MARY

All kidding aside, Jake, you really ought to. You needs them now you're starting back to work.

JACOB

(slipping on the glasses) I don't require glasses.

MARY

Don't you?

JACOB
(crosses back to his chair, sits, reads) No. How often must I tell you? I got along without 'em this long.

MARY
What's you wearing mine for then?

JACOB
Making out the fine print.

MARY
Yes, like the headlines. And you calls *me* vain.

JACOB
Besides, I owns my own pair, if you ain't t'rowed 'em out already like you t'reatened to.

MARY
What? Those old t'ings you bought off the counter at Woolworth's? I wouldn't trust you to cross the street with those on.

JACOB continues to read. Pause.

JACOB
(musing aloud) Is that the same Sam Morgan, I wonders?

MARY
Who'd you say?

JACOB
Sam Morgan. "Suddenly, at St. Joseph's Hospital, on Wednesday, January 10, beloved husband of . . ."

MARY
(snatches the newspaper from his hands) That's enough of that! What's wrong with you, lately?

JACOB
Give that back. I wasn't reading the obituaries.

MARY

No? What was it—the comic strip?

JACOB

I just happened to glance t'rough it. Give it here. I t'ought Dot might've been mentioned.

MARY

How? She only passed away yesterday. It was too late for Saturday's paper. She'll be in tomorrow's, if Wiff ain't forgot to phone it in. *(She hands back the newspaper and crosses back behind the ironing board.)*

JACOB

Don't be foolish, Mary, the funeral parlour does that. And listen here, you let up on Wiff, you hear? "Blessed are the merciful", or is that one not in the same Bible you reads?

MARY

If I had my way, he wouldn't put his foot in the door.

JACOB

Well, Wiff's me oldest friend, and he's welcome in this house anytime, day or night.

MARY

He don't deserve your sympathy, and he won't get mine. As if his philandering wasn't bad enough . . .

JACOB

By the Jesus, Mary, I wouldn't wish you for an enemy. You'm some hard case at times. Wouldn't move you with a winch, once your mind's set. *(He returns to his newspaper. Pause.)*

MARY
Still can't believe she's gone . . .

JACOB
Sam Morgan. Ain't that a kick in the ass. We worked together a few years back, Mary. You minds him.

MARY
Don't recall.

JACOB
Yes, you do so, now. Second cousin to Skipper Dick Chard from Buttercove. Married a Drudge from Tickle Harbour.

MARY
Sam Morgan?

JACOB
Had a glass eye.

MARY
Oh?

JACOB
A blue one. We was mates together over at Canada Packers, hanging doors. What a great one for fun, Sam. He'd sit on the crowded streetcar mornings, up to his old devilment, his eye in backwards . . .

MARY
And he passed away?

JACOB
Wednesday. They buried him yesterday, it says. Mount Pleasant Cemetery. And I never knowed he was sick, even. Never got a chance to pay my respects. *(slight pause as he scans the obituary)* Don't say what he died of. But knowing Sam, I dare say he choked to death on his own eye. He'd pop it in his mouth for fun.

MARY
Yes, and two guesses who egged him on.

JACOB
Just fifty, Mary. Fifty.

MARY
Is that all he was? That's young, fifty.

JACOB
Two years younger than us.

MARY
Look, boy, put down that old newspaper and get dressed.
You're getting on my nerves. Go on.

JACOB
(stands, crosses into living-room, looks for photo album) Strong as a
sled-horse, Sam. He'd pick up a keg of nails and lug it under
his arm.

MARY
Is it worth it to iron your old workshirt for tomorrow?

JACOB
We was in the Church Lads' Brigade together, years and
years ago . . . *(finds the photo album in a drawer)* Don't we have a
snapshot here somewhere? I'm sure of it . . . The two of us in
our little blue pillbox hats, khaki puttees, and blue breeches
. . . "Fight the good fight." That was our motto.

MARY
Jake?

JACOB
Friends dropping like flies . . . First your sister, and now . . .

MARY
(sharply) Jake!

JACOB
What? *(He crosses to the arm-chair and sits looking through album.)*

MARY
You don't listen. You want your workshirt ironed or not?

JACOB
Well, speak up if you wants an answer. Yes, and I needs a clean pair of woollen socks as well. Is my long underwear clean?

MARY
I bought you a new pair at Eaton's.

JACOB
Did you take the pins out?

MARY
I did. *(chuckling)* That won't happen again. *(slight pause)* Jake?

JACOB
What?

MARY
(crosses to JACOB) About tomorrow . . .

JACOB
What about it?

MARY
If you're doing this on my account . . .

JACOB
Oh, for Christ's sake, don't start in on that again.

MARY
I'm only t'inking of you, boy.

JACOB

Well, you just tell the Honeydew you'm quitting on Friday. There's no need of both of us working.

MARY

But the doctor said . . .

JACOB

I don't care what he said. I've been off seven weeks, and that's long enough.

MARY

Another month or two won't make no difference . . .

JACOB

Never had much use for doctors the best of times. Still don't.

MARY

(crosses back to the ironing board) No, except when it's me that's sick.

JACOB

He don't understand what it's like, not working. How could he? Never done a honest day's work in his life. So don't mention him again.

MARY

All right, I won't.

JACOB

Takes out a tonsil or two and calls it work. He don't know what work is. Christ, he can't remove a wart without he burns it off with acid. Even Dot could do better than that. Why, you'd rub your hand across her fur coat and the wart'd drop off within a week or two—without Blue Cross.

MARY

Yes, well, some good it done her, poor soul . . .

JACOB

As much good as those goddamn butchers with their knives.

MARY

Well, if Dot had only listened to the doctor and had her check-ups, she might be alive today. *(pause)* Don't seem fair, do it? How someone that gentle could die in such pain.

JACOB

(slight pause) Mary?

MARY

What, boy?

JACOB

I ain't had a single pain in weeks, Mary. Not a single pain.

MARY

No? I heard you the other night . . . groaning. What was that?

JACOB

Heartburn.

MARY

Was it?

JACOB

Heartburn, I tells you.

MARY

If you says so . . .

JACOB

That damn margarine again. And don't put any on my sandwiches. If you does, I'll toss my lunchpail and all to the sparrows. And they'll suffer. *(pause)*

MARY

(placing iron on counter) What's the forecast say? Did you look?

JACOB

(into his newspaper) Ten above.

MARY

How cold's that if you're high up?

JACOB

Ten below, perhaps.

MARY

That cold? Perhaps you'll work inside.

JACOB

Perhaps.

MARY

Might they let you off early?

JACOB

(teasing her) The wind's the worst, Mary. Seen a young lad one time, lugging a pane of glass; the wind took it like a sail and off he went . . .

MARY

(dismantles the ironing board, crosses to the cupboard, puts it away) T'anks for telling me, boy. I needed to hear that. Got any more good news you're keeping back?

JACOB

Fifteen stories below . . .

MARY

Enough. I'll have bad dreams tonight.

JACOB

Don't be foolish. I ain't some young Eye-talian the first day on the job, tripping over his own toes.

MARY puts the bushel basket on the counter, puts the ironing inside it.

MARY

No, you could've been a carpenter foreman today, if you'd a mind to . . .

JACOB

Well, I ain't, so forget it . . .

MARY

You was asked often enough.

JACOB

I couldn't do figures.

MARY

You can read a blueprint, can't you? And you measures better with your eye than most can with a slide rule. You just don't t'ink enough of yourself, Jake. You never did.

JACOB

Look, the truth is I'm fortunate to be working. How many companies you suppose wants to hire you, once word gets around you got a bad heart?

MARY

You could've been more, Jake.

JACOB

What odds? I'm a damn good carpenter. Ain't that enough? I ain't cut out to be a slave driver.

Enter BEN, dressed in his dark suit. JACOB quickly removes MARY's glasses, reads his newspaper.

BEN

Uncle Wiff not here yet?

MARY

Not yet, my son. *(She crosses to BEN.)* Well, look at you. Look, Jake. All growed up. Don't you look smart. I see you borrowed one of your father's ties. *(JACOB reacts.)* You looks good in a shirt and tie. Don't he, Jake?

JACOB

Just make sure you leaves the knot in, that's all.

MARY

(trying to laugh it off) He still ain't learned to tie a knot yet. Can you beat that? Still relies on your brother to do it for him.

JACOB

At least Billy takes an interest in the family. Don't find him gallivanting all over the country.

MARY
(*changing the subject quickly*) Suit still fits, I see . . .

BEN
Yeah, but the ass is shiny. Will there be many people there?

MARY
Oh, I wouldn't worry. No one will see that, I'm sure.

JACOB
(*rises, puts away album*) No, his father's the only one he shows his ass to. Well, you may not have me around much longer to run down. (*He starts up the stairs.*) Once the heart goes . . . (*He exits.*)

BEN
(*to MARY*) The what? . . . (*calling up the stairs*) Wait a minute. What are you talking about? Dad!

But JACOB has gone. A beat or two. BEN turns and looks at MARY, who enters the kitchen. He follows her.

What'd he mean—the heart? What's he talking about? Is there something wrong with his heart? Mom?

MARY
Sit down, Ben. And don't be angry with me.

BEN
No, I'll stand . . .

MARY
Suit yourself. (*She sits, looks at her hands.*) I've wanted to tell you ever since you walked in tonight, but I was afraid you'd come down on me for not telling you before. (*She turns and looks at BEN.*)

BEN
I'm listening . . .

MARY

I lied to you, Ben. Your father never strained his back. That wasn't why he was in the hospital.

BEN

What was it then?

MARY

A heart attack.

BEN

A heart at—?

MARY

Back in November. And he wasn't in the hospital for just a week. It was more like a month.

BEN

Why didn't you tell me?

MARY

I had my reasons.

BEN

What reasons? What possible reason could there be? Didn't you think I cared?

MARY

Wasn't that at all. I just didn't want you here.

BEN

What do you mean, you didn't want me here? He's my father, isn't he?

MARY

Yes, and he's my husband, and he comes first, now. I do what's best for him, not you. For *him*, do you understand?

BEN

So? What's that got to do with it?

MARY

What would you've done, Ben, had I told you the truth? You'd've been the first on the plane.

BEN

So?

MARY

Well, I wasn't about to risk losing him on account of you. How was I to know what might happen if you showed up at the hospital?

BEN

I wouldn't have fought with him, for Christ's sake. Don't you know me better than that?

MARY

It wasn't you I was worried about, it was him. He wasn't supposed to move, even. What if he saw you and went into one of his rages? What then? As it was, he had two more attacks in the hospital that almost finished him.

BEN

(angrily) Wait a minute. You mean he almost died and you didn't tell me?

He turns away to the sink, stands for a moment with his back to MARY. Then suddenly, violently, he smashes his fist into the cupboard door. He leans over the sink, motionless.

MARY

You got his temper, all right. I hoped you'd be different . . . *(pause)*

BEN

(turning) How'd it happen?

MARY

Oh, it was stupid, stupid. We was lugging that fridge down off the back of the truck, just the two of us. I wish to goodness I'd never heard tell of it. Stupid old fridge.

BEN
Why didn't you have it delivered?

MARY
We could've, if he'd just waited another day. But no, no, he's got no patience. Had to have it right away, that very afternoon. It was too much for just the two of us. I ain't that strong, and he knowed it. He had most of the weight on his end . . .

BEN
(crosses to MARY) All right, Mom, it's not your fault.

MARY
The fridge was my idea . . .

BEN
You couldn't know . . .

MARY
. . . He just let it drop, suddenly, and went inside. Stretched out on the chesterfield. Not a word out of him. I had no idea what was wrong, no idea. Started to frighten me, just lying there with his eyes closed, the beads of sweat on his forehead.

BEN
Didn't you call the doctor?

MARY
He wouldn't hear tell of it, at first. I had to practically t'reaten him, and when the doctor showed up, there was no way he was going to the hospital.

BEN
That figures.

MARY
"I ain't going!" he said. "You'll have to drag me! I wants to die in me own bed!" All because he had no clean underwear . . .

BEN
Jesus.

MARY

Oh, I'm glad you wasn't here, my son. He'd never've wanted you to see him carried out, shivering, on a stretcher, all wrapped in blankets. It was all I could do not to turn away my head. He looked so *puzzled* . . .

BEN

How could it happen, Mom? I mean he's not like other men. He's so strong.

MARY

Was, Ben.

BEN

Christ, when we were growing up, he'd make fun of us, Billy and me, if we got a blister. Like it was a sign of weakness or something.

MARY

Imagine then what this's done to him, a man that proud of his health and strength. Always wore it like some men wear a medal. T'ought he'd have it always like the colour of his eyes. *(slight pause)* I t'ink he's frightened, now. Frightened and ashamed.

BEN

Ashamed? Of what?

MARY

He can't keep up with others, even men his own age, and he knows it. I t'ink it preys on his mind like an insult. *(slight pause)* I never wanted you here, my son, but since you is, perhaps you can talk some sense into him, without getting into a row. Before it's too late.

BEN

What do you mean "too late"?

MARY

I'm frightened to death, Ben. He starts back to work tomorrow. Wiff got him a job. He ain't ready.

BEN
Is that what the doctor says?

MARY
He warned him against it.

BEN
Can't you talk to him?

MARY
I've tried my best, but he t'inks I'm in league with the doctor. Perhaps you'll have better luck.

BEN
He'd never listen to me, Mom. We'd just get in another argument.

MARY
It's worth a try, ain't it? Do it for me. I'm at my wit's end, my son.

BEN
What the hell's he trying to do, Mom—kill himself?

MARY
Don't say that.

BEN
Well, Christ, that's what it looks like.

MARY
No, Ben, it's my fault. I made the mistake of mentioning my legs was hurting. All that standing at work. That's all the excuse he needed. The very same night he was on the phone to Wiff. *(Doorbell rings.)* Speak of the devil, that's him now. *(She crosses to the foot of the stairs.)* Jacob!

JACOB
(off) What?

MARY

Wiff's here! Hurry up! Answer the door!

JACOB

(off) What's wrong with *your* two feet? I'm dressing.

MARY

(as she crosses back to the counter and gets the bushel basket, to BEN)
I t'ought he only took a minute? You answer it. *(She crosses
back to the archway.)* I'm going upstairs. I don't want to see his
ugly face.

BEN

(crossing to archway) Mom, did you tell Billy about the heart
attack?

MARY

Yes . . . He came to the hospital.

BEN

Great. No wonder Dad's so pissed off. He thinks I knew, too,
right?

MARY

What could I do, Ben? He'd have t'ought it strange if I hadn't
let both you know.

*She exits upstairs. Doorbell rings again. BEN crosses out into the
hallway and answers the door.*

BEN

(off) Hello, Uncle Wiff.

WIFF

(off) Who's that? Is that you, Billy?

BEN

(off) Ben.

WIFF

(off) Ben? No. Is that you, Ben?

He follows BEN into the hall. WIFF is dressed in an overcoat and dark suit. He wears a black fedora with a red feather in the brim, and has the red nose of a drinker.

Well, for crying out loud I never recognized you, duckie, it's been so long. Your old Uncle Wiff never recognized you. When'd you get in?

BEN

Just a while ago. I flew home.

WIFF

Jacob must be some t'rilled, I dare say. *(He takes off his rubbers.)* You all alone?

BEN

No. Mom and Dad're upstairs. *(WIFF removes his hat, places it on the banister.)* I was sorry to hear about Aunt Dot, Uncle Wiff.

WIFF

Terrible, my son, terrible. And just when we was planning a trip home this summer. *(He crosses to the chesterfield.)* Our first since we left. Even got the old car fixed . . . Oh, well, Dot's better off now. This life was too much for her. Perhaps the next'll be a little kinder . . . *(He sits on the chesterfield.)*

BEN

Wold you like a drink, Uncle Wiff?

WIFF

No, I don't dare touch it. Your mother'd crown me, duckie, if she caught me . . . You say she's upstairs? Your Uncle Wiff'll have a whiskey then, as long as you makes it quick. And straight.

BEN enters the kitchen, gets the whiskey and a glass from the cupboard, pours a drink. WIFF takes a mickey from the inside pocket of his overcoat and takes a quick drink, slips it back.

How long you home for, Ben? For good?

BEN
No. Just till the funeral.

WIFF
Oh? A good excuse to come home, eh, my son? *(BEN doesn't answer. WIFF rises, removes his coat and scarf, hangs them over the banister.)* Too bad you couldn't stay a spell longer. Your father could do with some help now. He ain't at all well. Scares me sometimes to look at him.

BEN
Yeah, I've noticed.

WIFF
(crosses to archway) A lot of changes in two years, boy . . . Even the cold bothers him, now. *(BEN returns from the kitchen and hands WIFF his drink.)* And I can recall times he'd find fun with it all, even the cold . . . Did he ever tell you the time back home me and him was in Holyrood?

BEN
(sitting in the arm-chair) No, I don't think so.

WIFF
What a bugger of a cold night that was. Freeze your poor pecker off. We drove into this little town one night in the winter, Jake and me. Just boys, the two of us. I had my father's old coal truck. Checked into the first hotel we saw —what we called back home a "baseball hotel".

BEN
What's that?

WIFF
A baseball hotel? That's a pitcher on top of the dresser and a catcher underneath. *(BEN laughs.)* Holyrood's a Catholic town, and the room we had was all decked out in religious pictures of bleeding hearts. Never seen so many in

me life. Just a little room with a bare bulb hanging down over the bed. And the last t'ing we seen before I reached up and switched off the light was this big picture of Jesus on the far wall. There he was, poor old Jesus, with his halo and crown of t'orns and this big red heart dripping down on his white gown, with a flame shooting out the top of the heart, and him standing there with his arms stretched wide open—*(he gestures)*—and it was that cold in our room, duckie—and Jacob'll back me up—it was that cold that in the morning when we looked up, Jesus had his hands over his ears like this. *(He demonstrates.)*

BEN
(laughing) Christ!

WIFF
Yes, that's right, my son—poor old Jesus Christ! *(then—seriously)* Oh, he ain't the same man, Ben, since the night you run off. I can testify to that. And what a state he was in at the time. Worse than your mother. Never ate for days. I doubt he slept a wink till he knowed where you was.

BEN
He shouldn't have beat me, Uncle Wiff. I warned him.

WIFF
Forget it. You're a bigger man than that, duckie. Make up. Take your Uncle Wiff's advice. Stay home and give him a hand. He's worked hard for you all his life. You might do the same in return. *(BEN says nothing.)* Some sons would, gladly.

BEN
I don't want to live at home any more. I like being on my own. He'll be all right.

WIFF
Will he? Have you taken a good look at him, lately? Have you, my dear? A close look? That's a man walking in the valley of the shadow. Mark my words.

BEN
Then why'd you get him the job? Did you have to?

WIFF
Wait a minute, now, duckie, wait a minute. *(He sits on the chesterfield.)* I ain't denying he wants to work. Your Uncle Wiff never said that, did he? All I'm saying is he oughtn't to. He ain't in no shape.

BEN
Did you tell him that?

WIFF
Bless your heart, I did so. I advised him to wait a few months, after he's more rested up . . .

BEN
So what do you think I should do?

WIFF
He might listen to reason, if he t'ought you was staying home. That might do the trick.

Enter JACOB. WIFF quickly passes his glass to BEN.

JACOB
Wiff, my son, how is you? Still holding up?

WIFF
Oh, as good as can be expected, duckie. As good as can be expected.

JACOB
(to BEN) Where's your manners? Get your uncle a drink.

MARY
(entering, sitting on the far end of chesterfield, away from WIFF) He don't want a drink, and neither does you. Have a grain of sense. Look what happened yesterday.

JACOB

(ignoring MARY) Wiff?

WIFF

No, my son, I'm off it for Lent, as the old man used to say. Off it for Lent.

JACOB

Suit yourself. I t'ink I'll have a quick one. *(He enters the kitchen, pours himself a drink.)* Been down to Jerrett's yet, Wiff?

WIFF

Just come from there, duckie. Saw Dot for a few minutes.

MARY

Oh? How do she look?

WIFF

Lovely, maid, lovely. Never know it was the same person. Just like she's sleeping.

JACOB

Did you see our flowers?

WIFF

I did, bless your heart. T'anks ever so much. They's lovely. Even the Oakwood Hotel sent a big wreath signed by all the waiters.

MARY

Not surprising. You're the best customer they ever had.

BEN

Mom, for Christ's sake . . .

MARY

Even Dot's dying couldn't keep him out on a Saturday afternoon.

WIFF

Must be our time of life, Mary. Flowers don't smell of the fields, lately . . . only of the funeral parlour . . . of death. *(pause)*

MARY

What dress did you settle on?

WIFF

What dress . . . ?

MARY

Wasn't a black one, was it? You know how she felt about black.

WIFF

No, maid, wasn't black . . .

MARY

Did any of her dresses fit her? I wouldn't t'ink they would, all the weight she lost.

WIFF

Well, one did, Mary. Just one, my dear . . .

MARY

Which one?

WIFF

Well . . . *(He rises, moves nervously behind the chesterfield.)*

MARY

No, don't tell me, Wiff. *(She stands.)* If you done what I t'ink you done I'll wring your neck for sure. That's a promise.

JACOB enters with his drink and glances from WIFF to MARY.

JACOB

What in Christ's name's going on now? Can't I step out of the room for two minutes, Mary?

MARY

Oh, I could murder him, I could. Guess what he's went and done, Jake? You won't believe this. Not in a million years.

JACOB
What?

MARY
Stuck Dot in her wedding dress. After what I told him Dot said.

JACOB
Did you, Wiff?

WIFF
That was the custom, Mary. You knows yourself. Why, the day we was married your poor mother said to Dot, "Now, me baby *(rhymes with abbey)* pack your dress away, that's for your funeral."

MARY
And what was it I told you Dot said just before she died? Her very last words: "Don't let Wiff bury me in my wedding dress."

BEN sits on sofa, lights a cigarette.

WIFF
She never knowed what she was saying. Mary. She never meant that, for crying out loud. That wasn't Dot speaking. Not my Dot.

MARY
No? How would you know? Was you there? Here I is, trying to keep my husband alive at all costs, and you ain't got two minutes to give to a dying woman! *(She enters the kitchen, sits at the table.)*

JACOB
Leave my name out of it. *(then)* She's just upset, Wiff. Pay her no mind.

WIFF follows MARY into the kitchen.

WIFF

Look, Mary . . .

MARY

You just never loved her, Wiff, or you'd've made it to the hospital.

WIFF

That's a lie, Mary. I loved Dot, and don't you say I didn't. And once she loved me, too.

JACOB sits in the arm-chair.

By Jesus, there was a time I couldn't pass her chair without she'd reach out and touch me. And I was the same. I couldn't get close enough. I would've crawled down and lived inside her bowels. We was the perfect pair . . .

MARY

You took up with the boarder. That's what ruined it. And after Dot treated that girl like a daughter . . .

WIFF

I never looked at another woman, including Marie, till Dot went t'rough the change of life. Wouldn't have a t'ing to do with me, after that. Too tired, she'd say. Always tired . . .

MARY

All right, but was it too much trouble to sit with her till she went? You could've done that much.

WIFF

For crying out loud, Mary, I was on my way to the hospital, no odds what you believes. I wanted to say good-bye.

MARY

You wanted a whiskey more.

WIFF

I just stopped off at the Oakwood for a minute. For a quick one, I told myself.

MARY

You might've waited.

WIFF

No, duckie, I needed a good stiff drink right then, that's all there was to it. I'd been down to that hospital night after night for six weeks, watching her waste away to not'ing . . . hoping every day would be her last. I could hardly bear to look at her . . . One quick glass of Scotch. Should've only took two minutes, if that.

MARY

Why didn't it, then?

WIFF

Why? If you're ready to listen, I'll tell you why . . . I had my first whiskey, and no sooner had I drunk it than somet'ing came back to me so clear . . . *(He sits.)* The first time Dot and me ever met. T'irty-five years ago. Me on my way down to the coal shed to unload the steamer, her on her way to the church to light the fire. How it all came back, suddenly, sitting at that table. That dark road, the stars still out, and me with my flashlight and lunchpail, no older than Ben. And who comes tripping along the road towards me, but Dot, the beam of her flashlight bouncing and swinging. I puts the light in her young face, and for a moment I don't recognize her, she's blossomed out that much in the time I was away in Boston . . . "Is that you, Dot Snow?" And she laughs. I'd forgot how gentle laughter could be. "Is that you, Wiff Roach?" Well, duckie, I never made it to the coal shed that morning. No, by God, I never. And my father couldn't have dragged me, had he kicked me ass all the way with his biggest boots. I walked her up the road, instead, and we sat in her family pew till the sun come up. Two months later we was married. You remembers, Mary. You was the bridesmaid. *(slight pause—WIFF stands)* So that's how come I never made it to the hospital yesterday. I had another whiskey to ease the pain I was feeling, and a t'ird because the second never helped . . . So if you wants to hurt me, Mary, you go right ahead, my dear, but you're too late . . . and not'ing you can ever say or do will make me feel any worse than knowing what

Dot and me once had and what it come to in the end, without either one of us ever knowing why ... *(He sits again.)* And that's why I wants her buried in her wedding dress, if you must know, in spite of what she said at the last. What she wanted in those days past is just as real to me as what she wanted yesterday. Nor do it have the same sadness, Mary, not the same sadness at all ...

MARY turns to WIFF. Slow fade to black. Music.

Scene Two

Lights up. Two hours later. MARY rushes in, followed by BEN. She removes her coat and thrusts it at BEN, who hangs it up. She crosses into the kitchen, fills the electric kettle, plugs it in.

BEN
(removing his coat, hanging it up) Quit it, Mom. *(He enters the living-room.)* How long you going to keep this up? You didn't speak once all the way home.

MARY
No, and you don't deserve to be spoken to. And the same goes for your father.

BEN crosses to the chesterfield, sits reading a magazine.

What'd you let him get in a row for?

BEN
What do you mean let him? I didn't let him.

MARY
Didn't you see it coming? Couldn't you stop it?

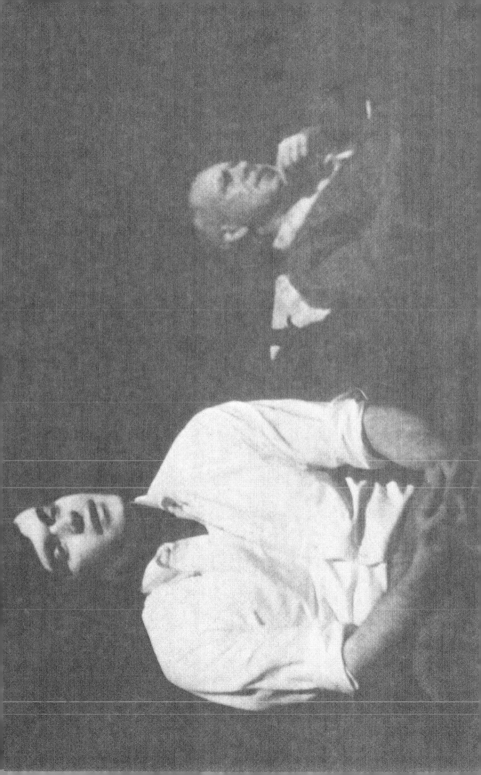

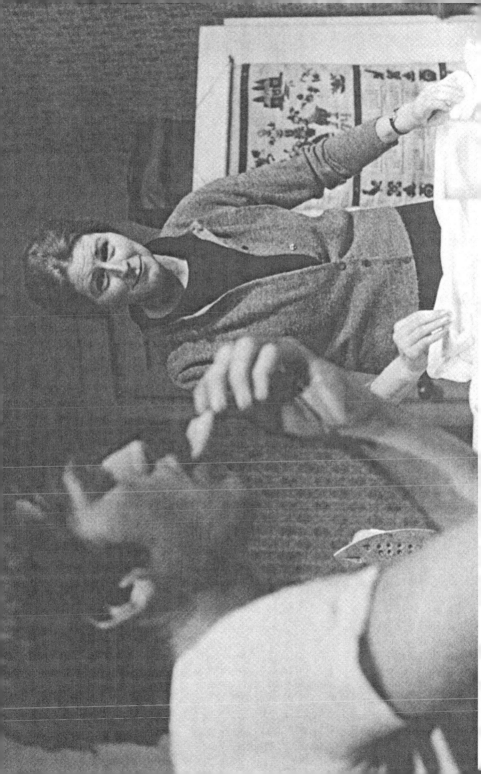

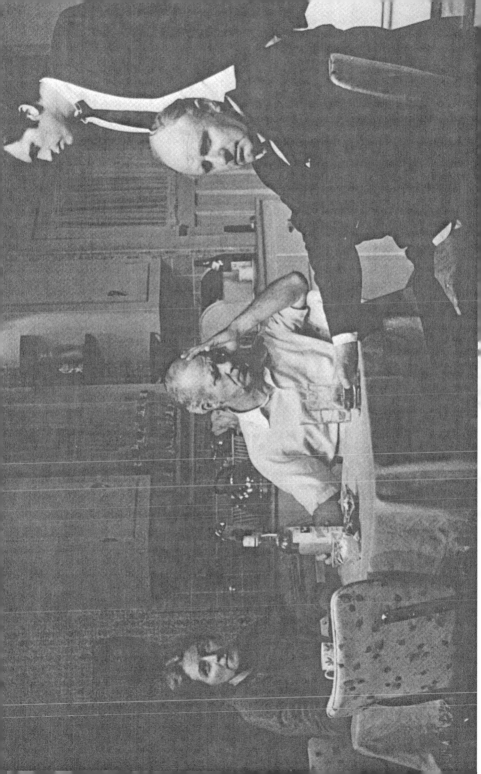

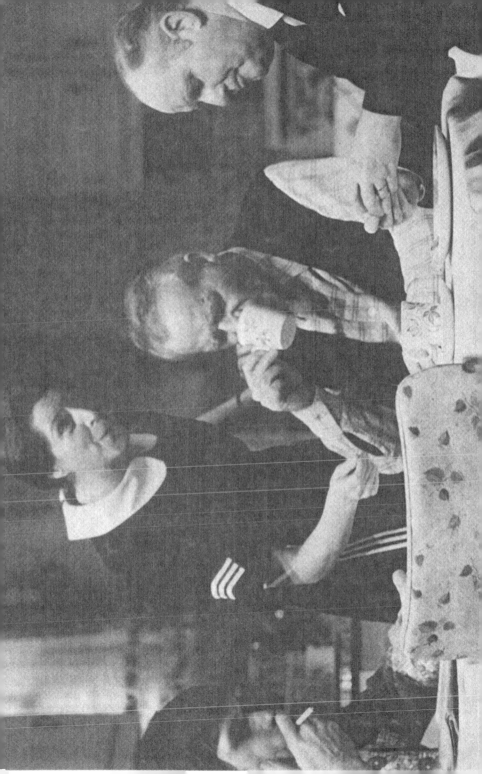

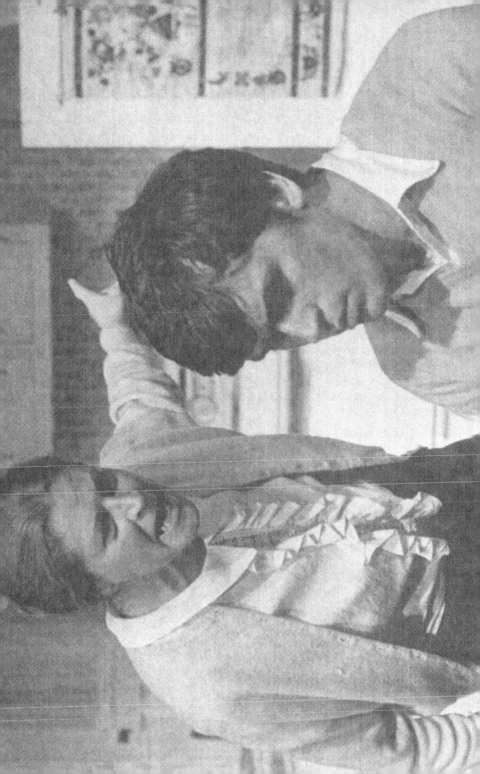

BEN

How? I was ten feet away talking to somebody. I still don't know what happened. He was talking to Uncle Wiff and some other guy . . .

MARY

Ike Squires.

BEN

Who?

MARY

Your father never had much use for him, even back home.

BEN

Anyway, the next thing I knew this guy was running out the front door with Dad after him.

MARY

Well, he's just lucky Ike can run faster than him. Wouldn't that be a nice sight—two growed men going to it on the street? What'll people say, for goodness sake?

BEN reaches over and flicks on the radio. A late-night jazz piece plays.

BEN

Actually, it was pretty funny . . . *(He laughs.)*

MARY

(crosses to archway) Funny? There was not'ing funny about it. And you're just as bad as him, if you laugh. That only encourages him. *(She returns to the kitchen.)*

BEN

Come on, Mom, where's your sense of humour? Look at it this way . . . Who else do you know would pick a fight inside a funeral parlour?

MARY

Yes, and my poor sister lying dead a few yards away. What a

sin. *(slight pause)* I stood there tonight looking down at Dot
—and God forgive me—all I could t'ink about was perhaps
your father was next. *(She crosses to the archway.)* Did you speak
to him yet, like I asked you to?

BEN
No. Not yet.

MARY
Why not? He'll soon be off to bed.

BEN
I just haven't had a chance. I will, when he comes in from the
garage.

MARY
See that you do. *(crossing to BEN)* Oh, Ben, I've been some
uneasy, lately, I don't mind telling you. At night I've been
coming awake and listening for your father's breathing in the
dark. If I don't hear it, I gets frightened and jabs him in the
ribs with my elbow. If that don't wake him, I gets more frightened and snaps on the light. And on top of that, last night I
had a bad dream. Can't get it out of my mind.

BEN
Really? What was it like?

MARY
Not now. Your father might come in any second. Later. *(She
starts for the kitchen.)*

BEN
No. Come on, Mom. I'd like to hear it, okay? I've had a
strange one myself, lately.

MARY
(turns back to BEN) I took it for a warning, Ben. Like a bird in
the house . . . Death ain't always a pale rider on a pale horse,
my son. Sometimes . . . like last night . . . he's just a man
dressed all in black. Wearing a peaked cap and holding a
black lunchpail. Standing high on a rooftop . . . *(She pauses.)*

BEN
Yeah? Is that all?

MARY
It was windy, and the wind took his cap off, and he just stood
there staring out over the city . . . as though he was beside the
shore, looking out to sea for somet'ing lost . . .

*Stamping of feet is heard outside the kitchen door, and MARY re-
turns to the kitchen counter, just as JACOB enters, carrying his
rubbers. As he closes the door behind him, she picks up a cup and
saucer and turns. The cup falls to the floor and shatters.*

JACOB
That's one you won't t'row at me. *(He crosses to the hallway
closet.)*

MARY
The night ain't over yet, boy.

JACOB
(hanging up his coat, to MARY) At least she's speaking to me.

MARY
(as she sweeps up the broken cup) I oughtn't to, after the fool you
made of yourself tonight. Where did you t'ink you was—the
beer parlour?

JACOB
Go on with you. We had a few words, that's all.

*He enters the kitchen, crosses to the fridge. He removes a wedge of
cheese and cuts off a slice with his penknife.*

MARY
Words? Is that what you calls it? Well, I'd hate to be the one
has a conversation with you. *(She deposits the broken cup in the
garbage receptacle.)* What brought that on?

JACOB
Not'ing. I don't wish to talk about it.

MARY

Well, get out of the kitchen, then. Go in the other room. Ben wishes to speak to you.

JACOB

He do? What do he want?

MARY

How should I know? Go and find out.

JACOB

You come in with me, Mary.

MARY

Don't be silly. Go on. He won't bite. *(as JACOB picks up a newspaper off the top of the fridge)* And leave the paper right where it is. You won't need to hide behind that. *(pushing him towards the door)* Go on, I said.

As JACOB enters the living-room, BEN switches off the radio. JACOB removes his tie and hangs it over the banister. He looks at BEN's back a moment. Then he crosses behind the chesterfield to the window.

JACOB

Wonder how much Wiff paid for that casket? Bronze is the most expensive there is. Must've set him back two t'ousand, at least, wouldn't you say?

BEN

Probably more than that. *(slight pause)* Dad . . .

JACOB

(not hearing BEN) Back home we never had funeral parlours in my day.

BEN

No?

JACOB

No. When Father died, he was kept home in bed, and

somebody—mostly Mother and me—sat with him for the t'ree days, every hour. *(Out of his embarrassment he takes a pack of cigarettes from his shirt pocket, discovers it empty, then crosses to the arm-chair and sits.)* Some would keep their blinds drawn for months on end. Once the preacher preached a sermon saying what a sin it was to keep out the Light of God that way. *(BEN quickly offers his father a cigarette. JACOB takes one.)* T'anks. *(He breaks off the filter, and BEN lights the cigarette for him.)* They never embalmed in those days, either. And lots couldn't wait the t'ree days, let me tell you. Had to be buried sooner.

(Pause.)

BEN
How did your father die?

JACOB
Cancer, my son. Like Dot. He was only forty-six.

BEN
What was he like?

JACOB
Father? Oh, that depended on who crossed his path and what mood he was in. On good days he'd give you the bread out of his mouth. He was a hard man to know. Don't suppose many knowed him well, except Mother. She was the only one wasn't frightened of him. *(slight pause)* The first time they operated on him, four men had to hold him down on the kitchen floor. No morphine, no kind of pain-killer, just the knife and four men kneeling on his arms and legs. A ball of flesh as big as a marble popped out of his mouth and rolled across the floor. Never let out a whimper, just kicked and t'rashed. The cancer was in his mouth, you see, and Mother said she'd pick up teeth in the bedclothes weeks later. *(slight pause)* The night he died he was in such torment he reached up and took hold of the frame of the bed and bent the brass out of shape. Still never made a sound ... The doctor later said he never knowed how any normal man could've stood it without screeching out ...

BEN

Were you there?

JACOB

No. Mother told me later. She wouldn't let me near the room. Never wished me to see him, the shape he was in. At t'ree or four that morning she came out, rolling down her sleeves, and closed the door, and I knowed before she spoke he was gone, just the way she came out that way and closed the door . . . When I did see him, at last, after they'd made him up, he looked so small lying there in bed that I wondered to myself how I ever could've been so frightened of him, such a small man. In life, I'd never noticed that, how small he was . . . *(slight pause)* By the way, your Mother said you wished to speak to me.

BEN

Yeah, I do . . . *(He stands.)*

JACOB

What about?

BEN

Well, Mom told me you're going back to work tomorrow . . . and I was thinking . . .

JACOB

Don't waste your breath, my son. Did she put you up to this?

BEN

Put me up to what? You haven't let me finish. I'd like to stay home for a while if that's okay with you, and work.

JACOB

What'd you say? . . .

BEN

I said I'd like to stay home for a while and work. I mean, if you don't mind.

JACOB

Mind?

BEN

Maybe you don't want me here. It's your house.

JACOB

That ain't true, now. Your mother owns half. She's got as much say in the matter as I does. *(He stands.)* Did you mention this to her yet?

BEN

No.

JACOB

Good. Watch me surprise her. Mary, come in here quick. Hear the good news. *(to BEN)* She'll be some overjoyed, Ben. *(then)* Mary! *(He crosses to the archway.)* Drop what you'm doing and get in here before he changes his mind.

MARY

(crosses to the sink, deposits her cup) What is it?

JACOB

Hang onto your bonnet, Mary. You'll never believe what I just heard with my own two ears. You ready for this?

MARY

(crosses to JACOB) You won the Sweepstakes.

JACOB

Better. Your son wishes to stay home.

MARY

(to BEN) Oh?

JACOB

"Oh?" Is that all you can say is "oh?"

MARY

What was you expecting?

JACOB

I t'ought the least you'd do is jump and smack your hands. You does that much at the bingo. Didn't you hear me? He wishes to stay home for good.

BEN

For a while.

JACOB

For a while? What's the good of that? *(then)* All right. For a while.

MARY

(to BEN) What for?

JACOB

There she goes again. What does you mean "what for?" By the Christ, if you aint contrary.

MARY

Perhaps we'd be better off if he never, Jake.

JACOB

In the name of Christ, Mary, what's got into you?

MARY

Remember what we talked about earlier? Just the two of us?

JACOB

All right, my son, pack your bag, your mother don't want you here.

MARY

It ain't that.

JACOB

Well, what kind of a way is that to speak? *(crosses to BEN)* Look, this is *my* house, and there's a spare bedroom. You can come and go to please yourself. And neither your mother nor me will interfere. Will we, Mary? *(then)* Will we?

MARY says nothing.

Well, this calls for a drink. I'll break out the whiskey. Billy gave me a bottle for Christmas. *(He rushes off into the kitchen and pours two drinks, singing.)*

"Up and down the southern shore
Go to bed after supper
See the great big ugly t'ing
Go after Charlie Tucker"

(then) Don't go back on your word, now.

MARY

What's the idea, Ben? You was supposed to convince him not to work. What's staying home got to do with it?

BEN

I'm going to get a job, and he won't have to work. I just haven't told him yet.

MARY

So that's it. Well, my son, you'd better let him know what you intends. He might not go for it.

JACOB rushes back with the two drinks, hands one to BEN.

JACOB
Here you is, my son. Here's to us, to the t'ree of us. Down the
hatch. *(He drinks. BEN doesn't.)* This is some night, ain't it? Just
like old times. My only regret is poor Billy ain't here. *(slight
pause)* Why the long faces? Look at the two of you. What
gives? *(then)* Mary? . . .

MARY
You never let him finish, Jake. There's more. I t'ink you
ought to hear the rest of it.

JACOB
The rest of what?

Doorbell rings, then pounding on the door.

What's that? . . .

MARY
Someone's at the door.

BEN
I'll get it. *(He exits.)*

JACOB
(to MARY) At this hour? *(He crosses to the window, looks out.)*
Why, it's Wiff . . .

MARY
Wiff? What's he want?

JACOB
Now how should I know? *(He crosses into the hall.)*

MARY
Don't you dare give him anyt'ing to drink. We'll never get rid
of him.

*WIFF rushes in, holding his heart. BEN follows. WIFF is dressed
only in his suit. He is agitated, breathless, dishevelled, and shivering
from the cold.*

JACOB

Wiff, my son, what's wrong? What's you doing out like that?

WIFF

Let me catch my breath. I'm half froze . . .

JACOB

Who's after you, boy—the devil?

WIFF

No, duckie, Dot. *(He warms his hands on the radiator.)*

JACOB

(to MARY) What'd he say?

MARY

(her eyes on WIFF) Dot . . .

JACOB

Dot . . . ?

MARY

Has you been drinking, Wiff?

WIFF

No, bless your heart, I ain't been drinking. Nor will I touch another drop as long as I lives, if I lives to be two hundred. Not after tonight . . . *(He collapses on the chesterfield.)*

MARY

He must've been dreaming.

JACOB

How could he? We just dropped him off. He hardly had time to take off his coat.

WIFF

Close to t'ree t'ousand dollars, almost a year's salary, I paid for her funeral. And she calls me heartless. *(to BEN)* Your

Uncle Wiff's heartless. *(then grabbing BEN's drink)* Is you drinking that, duckie? I needs to calm my nerves, love.

MARY

(to herself) The shortest two hundred years I ever seen.

WIFF

What's she want to come after me for, for crying out loud. We had plenty of good times in the past . . . One time I come home drunk from the Union meeting and she'd locked me out. So I sat down on the steps and took a spell. All of a sudden up went the window overhead and down came a pan of cold water. I jumped halfway out in the road, with the fright. Then she come downstairs and let me in, laughing to beat the band . . .

JACOB

All right, boy. Tell us what happened.

WIFF

. . . Well, when I got home, duckie, I hung up my overcoat, switched on the basement light and went down to the furnace. Damn t'ing's been acting up, lately, clicking off when it shouldn't . . . and there she was, Dot, standing in the shadows beside the washing machine, as real as you or me.

MARY

Blessed God.

WIFF

Walked right up to me, love, wearing that old raggedy dressing-gown of hers.

JACOB

Mother saw Father about the house, weeks after he died.

WIFF

Oh, she laid right into me, Ben. The names she called your old Uncle Wiff. And I t'ought Dot never knowed a single one of them words, Jake. Said I ought to have tried to reach her when she was alive. Said I never cared enough. "Why'd you let it happen?" she said. "Why didn't you reach out?" Said she'd follow me the rest of my days for what I done . . . Well, duckie, I got out of there some quick, let me tell you. And when I looked back, she was starting up the stairs after me, crying to beat hell . . . That's when I took off out the door. I run all the way here.

JACOB

Don't you worry none, Wiff. We'll put you up. Plenty of room here.

MARY

Where will he sleep? Is you forgetting who's home?

BEN

I'll sleep on the chesterfield. He can have the bedroom.

MARY

Suit yourself. I'll get the blankets. *(She exits upstairs.)*

WIFF

I couldn't go back there, Jake. I'd die of fright, if I was to wake up in the middle of the night with Dot leaning over me, as much as I adored her . . .

JACOB

Say no more, Wiff. I understands. *(to BEN)* Bring in the bottle, will you, my son? *(BEN exits into the kitchen.)* What do you say to another drink, Wiff, old boy? Take the chill out of your bones.

WIFF

No, bless your heart, I had one already tonight. One's my limit, after this. *(then)* She always wanted a blue silk dress, and I was always too stingy. Oh, my son, I wish I had it all to do over . . .

BEN enters with the whiskey bottle and a glass for himself.

BEN
Uncle Wiff?

WIFF
Well, perhaps I'll have a drop after all. A little one, my dear.
(as BEN pours) Not too little . . .

MARY comes downstairs, carrying a pillow, sheets and blankets.

MARY
(as she deposits the bedclothes on the chesterfield) Before I forgets it,
Wiff, what was that row about tonight down at Jerrett's?
Jacob's too modest to tell.

JACOB
Won't sleep till you knows, will you, Mary? No mistake.

WIFF
Oh, 'twas not'ing, Mary. Ike was boasting how they made him
foreman.

JACOB
Foreman! Don't know his ass from a blueprint. He married
the superintendent's daughter. That's how he got the job.

WIFF
Jake took him down a peg or two, didn't you, duckie? T'ought
he'd come to his own funeral by mistake.

MARY
Not carpenter foreman, Wiff?

WIFF
Yes. T'inks he's King Shit, now.

MARY
On what job?

WIFF
Ours, my dear.

JACOB

What've I told you all these years, Ben? It's who you knows, not what you knows.

MARY

Oh, you fool! He'll work you ragged, just to get back. You've done it this time, boy.

JACOB

Go on with you. I'll crown him with a two-by-four if he so much as looks at me sideways.

MARY

Yes, you will so.

JACOB

Oh, won't I?

MARY

No, and I'll tell you exactly what you'll do, knowing you. You'll do whatever he tells you to do and do it twice as quick as you ought to and then ask for more. That's what you'll do. As if it wasn't bad enough before!...(*She sits on the chesterfield.*)

WIFF

Come to t'ink of it, Jake, Ike's a mean bastard when he's sore. He don't forget an insult, that one. Watch out for him, boy. He might try to get back at you.

MARY

How?

WIFF

Oh, I've seen it before, Mary, more than once. A foreman's got it in for you, he gives you the worst job there is.

MARY

Which is?

WIFF

Rigging beam bottoms and beam sides. You got to climb out along the steel with your toolbox.

BEN

How high are they up?

WIFF

Twenty floors.

JACOB

For Christ's sake, Wiff, what's you trying to do—frighten her?

WIFF

All right, my son, I won't say another word. But if I was you . . .

JACOB

Well, you ain't me, and that's that.

WIFF

No, but if I was, I knows what I'd do, duckie. I'd tell him where to shove it or I'd quit first.

JACOB

I won't do no such t'ing. Do you t'ink I'd let that little bastard get the best of me? That'd be the day.

MARY

(desperately) All right, but what does you want more? To get the better of Ike Squires or for Ben to stay home? You'd better make up your mind right now, Jake, 'cause you can't have it both ways, not this time. Can he, Ben?

JACOB

What's you talking about? *(to BEN)* You'm staying home, ain't you?

MARY
Tell him, Ben. Go on.

JACOB
You made a promise, now. Don't go back on your word.

BEN
Yeah, but you never let me finish, Dad. I wanted to stay home
so you wouldn't have to work. That's what I was getting at
before. Even Uncle Wiff thinks it's a good idea.

JACOB
(to WIFF) Oh, he do, do he? What is this, Wiff—a goddamn
conspiracy?

WIFF
Now don't take it the wrong way, my son, I wouldn't go behind your back. You've been looking kind of pekid, lately,
that's all I meant.

MARY
Yes. You've earned a good rest, Jake. Ben's young and strong.
Let him pitch in for a spell.

WIFF
Jesus, if I had a son . . .

MARY
Just till you gets a clean bill of health, Jake. Not a second
longer.

WIFF
For crying out loud, you're too good a man to be taking
orders from that arsehole.

BEN
And what do you care what he thinks of you?

WIFF
I'd give a week's pay to watch King Shit crawling out on that
cold steel with a heavy toolbox.

JACOB
(*chuckling*) Did you see him tonight? Couldn't move his ass quick enough, could he, Wiff? Lickety-split like a jack-rabbit.

MARY
Jake, please . . . Reconsider, won't you? Do it for me, if not for yourself.

BEN
I want to, Dad.

Pause.

JACOB
Oh, for Christ's sake, Mary, if it's that important to you . . . (*He crosses into the kitchen with his glass and gets the whiskey bottle.*)

MARY
You won't go in then?

JACOB
No, I won't go in. Satisfied? You got your own way, as usual.

MARY
T'anks, Jake. (*to BEN and WIFF*) Now you both heard that. (*to JACOB*) And I'm holding you to it.

BEN
I'll look for a job tomorrow.

MARY
Do that. (*to JACOB as she crosses into the kitchen and pours herself a tea*) And you and me can take it easy for a spell.

JACOB
You'm to quit the Honeydew next Friday, don't forget.

MARY
I will, I will.

JACOB

And see the doctor about those legs. *(He sits at the table.)*

MARY

I'll make an appointment. Oh, you was right, Jake, you was right, boy. This is a night to celebrate and give t'anks. Wouldn't you say, Wiff? In spite of Dot?

WIFF

I would, my dear, yes . . . *(He sits.)*

JACOB

But it's only for a short spell, Mary. Get that t'rough your head. A few weeks.

MARY

Until the doctor says . . .

JACOB

No. Until Ben goes. *(BEN nods to MARY.)* Believe it or not Mary, I was looking forward to going back to work. That's somet'ing you just don't seem to understand, even after all these years . . .

MARY

I do, Jake.

JACOB

No, you don't. What am I supposed to do—slouch about the house growing fat and lazy? I'm only fifty-two. What have I got to live for without my work? You tell me that, Mary, if you can. What have I got to live for?

He pours WIFF another drink as the lights fade slowly to black.

ACT TWO

Scene One

Early next morning. On the kitchen table are two empty whiskey bottles and three glasses. One of the glasses still contains a little whiskey. There is also an ashtray overflowed onto the table.

In the living-room a song plays softly on the radio. The chesterfield has not yet been made up, and the sheets and blankets are tangled. BEN's pyjama bottoms are tossed carelessly over the arm-chair.

At rise, BEN is beside the fridge, drinking thirstily from a bottle of orange juice. He wears pyjama tops and blue jeans. He is barefoot. When he has drunk enough, he replaces the bottle and closes the fridge.

MARY
(off) Jake, is that you down there?

BEN
No, he went out, Mom. It's me.

MARY
(off) Take the butter out of the fridge, will you, my son? And plug in the kettle.

BEN does, as WIFF, freshly scrubbed, comes down the stairs and enters the kitchen.

WIFF
Hello, my precious. How's your head this morning? Care for some breakfast? *(He begins to prepare himself scrambled eggs and toast.)*

BEN
No, thanks. I couldn't look at food. *(slight pause)* Uncle Wiff?

WIFF
What can I do for you, love?

BEN
You ever have the same dream over and over?

WIFF
Yes, but I wouldn't dare tell you, you'd t'ink for certain your Uncle Wiff belonged in a cage. For years it was always me and Veronica Lake ... Ah, my son, we're odd creatures. For months after Dot lost interest in me, I never looked at another woman, and yet when me and her was most happy, I wanted to drive the boots home to every beautiful woman in the street ...

Just then MARY comes down the stairs dressed in her 'Honeydew' uniform. She is spraying with a can of lilac air freshener. BEN enters the living-room.

MARY
Morning, my son.

BEN
Morning, Mom. *(He sits on the chesterfield and slips on his socks and boots.)*

MARY
Morning, Wiff.

WIFF
Mary.

MARY circles the living-room spraying, then enters the kitchen and sprays.

MARY
You don't have to do that, Wiff. I'll make your breakfast. Sit down, boy.

WIFF

No, bless your heart, I can do it myself. I ain't helpless.

MARY

Wiff?

WIFF

Yes, my dear?

MARY

T'anks for last night. Jake'll listen to you before he will to me.

WIFF

Oh, don't t'ank me, love. It was all Ben's doing. Jake'd agree to leprosy to keep him around. You and me had little to do with it.

MARY, smiling, deposits the can on top of the fridge and returns to the living-room.

MARY

How'd you sleep?

BEN

Not too good.

MARY

Well, your first night back, that's to be expected. You're used to your own bed, now.

BEN

It wasn't the bed, Mom.

MARY

Hardly slept myself.

BEN

(as he helps MARY fold the sheets and blankets) How come? I thought you'd sleep okay last night.

MARY

No. Your father kicked and twisted all night. Wonder I ain't black and blue, or scratched to pieces. Never cuts his toe-nails.

BEN

Where'd he go?

MARY

Out back. He's warming up the truck.

BEN

What for?

MARY

He drives me to work.

BEN

Oh.

MARY

Not that he needs to . . . I suppose he feels funny, still in bed with me off to work. *(The sheets and blankets are now folded.)* I'd better see what he's up to. He ought to've been in by now. *(then)* Wiff? Is Jake out back?

WIFF

One second, maid, I'll look.

As WIFF looks out the kitchen window, MARY folds BEN's pyjama bottoms neatly over the back of the arm-chair.

No, no sign of him, Mary. *(He returns to making his breakfast.)*

MARY

Where could he be at? *(She crosses to the living-room window, looks out.)* No, there he is, shovelling the sidewalk. Without gloves, as usual. *(She watches.)*

BEN

(crosses to the window) I'd've done that. Next time get me up okay?

MARY

No, leave it be. He's got to have somet'ing to do. *(quickly)* Don't let him see you . . .

BEN

Why not?

MARY

Look how he leans on his shovel . . .

BEN

He looks old, Mom. I noticed that last night. Smaller . . .

MARY

Come away, now, before he catches you. *(as she moves away from the window)* You want some breakfast?

BEN

No. Just a coffee. I'll get it. *(He follows MARY into the kitchen. As she cleans the table of the whiskey bottles, glasses and ashtray, he unplugs the kettle and makes himself a mug of instant black coffee.)* . . . Mom, remember that dream I mentioned? I had it again this morning, the same one.

MARY

Oh?

BEN

Yeah. I think it woke me. I haven't been able to shake it off.

MARY

Is it that bad, my son?

BEN

It never made any sense before I came home. I think it does now.

MARY

You any good at dreams, Wiff?

WIFF

Not me, maid. Dot was the one. *(He crosses to the table with his plate, sits.)*

BEN

It's always the same, Mom . . . I'm on a brass bed, a big brass bed like the one we had back home when I was a kid. Remember?

MARY

(to WIFF) He always t'ought it was gold. The way it shone.

BEN

Whatever happened to it?

MARY

Oh, we left it back in Bay Roberts, my son, along with all that other old junk we never knowed was antiques.

BEN

(as he sits at the table) . . . Anyway, the bed's sitting at a cross-roads, two dirt roads, and I can see a cliff behind me, and the sea beyond that.

MARY

Might be Conception Bay.

BEN

Except I'm the same age I am now. It's a beautiful day, summer, and I'm just lying there on the bed at this cross-roads, wide awake, looking up at the blue sky, the sun sparkling on the bedposts . . . Suddenly the sky's full of butterflies, all different colours, millions of beautifully coloured wings . . . and then . . .

MARY

Yes? *(She crosses to BEN.)*

BEN

Then two people without faces, a man and a woman . . .

MARY
A man and a woman?

BEN
Yeah, they come up one road and look at me and go down the
other ... and suddenly the sky's black, it's night, and the
butterflies become snowflakes, and I'm running, really scared
for some reason, stumbling along this snowy road, running
home, running like crazy, and all I know is that I have to get
home fast because ... *(He pauses.)*

MARY
(sitting) Because what, my son?

BEN
Because something ... terrible is happening there, and I
don't know what ... something terrible ...

*BEN and MARY stare at one another. A beat. Then JACOB enters
offstage and slams the door. He stamps his feet and begins to cough a
hacking cough.*

MARY
I wish he wouldn't smoke. Sometimes he can't catch his breath
when he goes outside.

WIFF
Another reason he shouldn't be working up high.

JACOB
(appearing in the hallway, wearing his coat and cap; he sniffs)
Goddam place smells of lilacs! *(He hangs up his coat and cap in
the closet.)*

MARY
Now if I hadn't sprayed, he would've complained it smelled of
cigarettes. Contrary as the day is long. *(to BEN)* Was he cross
before he went to bed last night?

BEN
No.

WIFF
He was telling jokes, love.

MARY
First t'ing he noticed when he opened his eyes this morning, was the venetian blinds in the bedroom was dusty. Done not'ing but complain ever since.

JACOB
(entering the kitchen) Ain't my breakfast ready yet? You've had all morning for Christ's sake.

MARY
(to BEN) What'd I say? *(to JACOB, as she rises)* No, and Wiff made his own. I just got downstairs.

JACOB
Wiff.

WIFF
Duckie.

MARY
Sit down, boy. I'm just making the tea.

She puts three tea bags into the teapot and pours in hot water. BEN takes the newspaper off the counter and spreads out the want ads on a corner of the table. JACOB watches him a moment.

JACOB
(to BEN) Well, you'm up bright and early this morning. Can't wait to step into my shoes. *(to WIFF)* Look at him. *(He remains standing.)*

BEN
(running his finger down the want ad columns) I couldn't sleep, that's all.

JACOB

Makes no bloody wonder, after last night. You keeps drinking like that, you'll have the d.t.'s. I t'ought you could put it away fast, Wiff.

BEN

Get serious. I only had a few.

JACOB

A few?

BEN

He drank two to my one, didn't he, Uncle Wiff?

WIFF

Leave me out of it, duckie.

JACOB

He calls that a few, Wiff. Picked up some fine habits out west, I see. Nineteen years old . . .

BEN

Twenty.

JACOB

Twenty, is it?

BEN

I'll be twenty-one soon.

MARY

All right, just stop it, the both of you. Stop it. What's you want for breakfast, Jake? Bacon and eggs?

JACOB

Home one night, and staggering off to bed . . .

MARY

Is you hungry or not?

JACOB

Hungry? How the hell would I be hungry? I lost my appetite the day I stopped working. A bird could live on less.

MARY

Well, sit down and have a cup of tea, at least. You're making me nervous.

JACOB

(sitting) I suppose you'm working Wednesday, Wiff?

WIFF

Oh, yes, boy. Sooner the better. Best t'ing for me right now. Too much time on my hands is no good. Allows you to t'ink too much . . .

JACOB

You can say that again, Wiff. I never could sit on my ass for very long, even when I was laid off. Feel every minute, if I ain't active. Every goddamn minute. *(He looks at BEN.)* Ain't that Saturday's paper?

BEN

Yeah.

JACOB

This is Monday. What's the good of Saturday's paper to you? Why don't you look at last summer's? *(BEN says nothing.)* What a way he goes about t'ings, Wiff. My Christ. And he went to university, too.

BEN

Lay off, will you? I'll get the other papers, later. It's not going to hurt if I look, is it?

JACOB

No, don't give me no heed, I'm uneducated.

MARY

(changing the subject, as she crosses to the table, puts down a cup of tea for JACOB and WIFF) I'm surprised the t'ree of you never slept in. It must've been late when you come to bed.

JACOB
Who said it was late?

MARY
I t'ought it was. I never heard you come to bed.

WIFF
It was only one, Mary.

MARY
That's late for Jake.

JACOB
It might've been, when I was working. Not now. I can stay up to all hours, now.

MARY
(changing the subject again) More coffee, Ben?

BEN
(looking curiously at JACOB) No, thanks, Mom.

JACOB
(to BEN) What's you staring at? Never seen me face before?

BEN
What's wrong with you this morning? All you've done is bitch.

MARY
(to herself, as she crosses back to the counter and pours her own tea) Worse than an old woman.

JACOB
(to BEN) I don't like to be spied on, for starters. Is that good enough?

MARY
That ain't what's bothering you. Own up to it.

BEN
Who was spying on you?

JACOB

The two of you.

MARY

Oh, we was not.

JACOB

Liar. I seen you at the window. Next you'll be telling me I'm blind. I ain't some specimen under glass, Mary.

MARY

Did I say you was?

JACOB

Then don't watch me like a goddamn hawk. *(then)* Tea's like bark.

MARY

Why don't you just come out with what's eating at you and get it over with?

JACOB

Eating at me? What in Christ's name could be eating at me, Mary? I've got it all to my liking, now.

MARY

Well, there's no need to put us all t'rough this. Next t'ing you'll take after Wiff.

WIFF

(quickly) I'm just going, my dear. Just on my way out the door. *(He half-rises but JACOB stops him with a gesture.)*

JACOB

How many men you suppose would leap at the chance not to work? Most would give their eye-teeth. Bet Wiff would, if Dot was still alive.

MARY

All right, I've took all I can. If you wants to go to work so bad, go . . . Go! . . . Did you hear what I said?

JACOB
(glancing at BEN) Ah . . .

MARY
I won't stop you this time, if this is how you intends to carry on. I can't take much more. I'll pack your lunchpail, if you likes. *(She steps to the fridge and takes down his lunchpail.)*

JACOB
You will, like hell! *(He jumps up, follows her, snatches the lunchpail from her hands, and smashes it on the floor.)* There! *(Silence. MARY bends down and picks up his lunchpail and opens it. She removes the thermos and shakes it. It rattles.)* Now see what you made me do! *(He rushes out to the hall closet.)* Can't leave well enough alone for a second, can you, Mary? My good t'ermos. *(He returns to the kitchen, struggling to put on his coat and cap.)*

MARY
Don't be foolish, boy. Where do you t'ink you're off to?

JACOB
Out. And I don't know when I'll be back—if ever. Find your own way to work.

He exits the kitchen door, slamming it behind him. MARY rushes after him.

MARY
(off) Jake! Wait! Your rubbers! . . . *(Slowly, MARY returns, closing the door. She walks to the counter. We hear the truck drive off. As she picks up her teacup . . .)* Well, I got my wish, didn't I . . . And now it's started . . .

BEN
What has?

MARY
What I was afraid of . . .

Slow fade to black. Music.

Scene Two

Lights up. Early the same evening. The kitchen table has been set for four. MARY is alone onstage, standing at the living-room window. The curtains are pulled aside slightly, and she stares out at the street. Finally, she draws the curtains, crosses and enters the kitchen, checks the oven.

MARY
(to herself) Where could he be to? *(Offstage, the front door opens and closes. MARY darts to the table, quickly scoops up the plates, and begins slowly and casually to reset the table, humming a little tune. BEN enters the hallway, carrying a book. He removes his things and crosses to the archway, thumbing his book. MARY, turning.)* Oh, it's you . . . I t'ought it might be your father.

BEN
Why? Isn't he home yet?

MARY
No.

BEN
What time is it?

MARY
Just after six. I'm worried sick. It ain't like him to miss his supper. He's always home at five sharp, no odds what.

BEN
I wouldn't worry, Mom. He'll be back. You know how he talks.

MARY
What if he had an accident with the truck? I'm afraid to turn on the radio, in case . . .

BEN
Look, you're getting all worked up for nothing. If anything did happen, they wouldn't put it on the radio before notifying us.

MARY
(returns and sits at the table) I've always knowed where he was, at all times. This is the first time I wouldn't know where to reach him in case of an emergency. The first time since we was married . . .

BEN
(crosses into kitchen) Is Uncle Wiff here?

MARY
No.

BEN
So maybe he's with him.

MARY
I t'ought of that. Did Wiff say where he was going to this morning?

BEN
No. *(then)* Yeah, wait a minute, he did. He said he was going to the cemetery to pick out a plot.

MARY
They might be at the Oakwood together. He may've dropped in for a beer and seen Wiff. He'd soon forget the time.

BEN
Why don't you phone?

MARY
No. He don't like that. Makes him feel foolish, he says, in front of the other men. Would you?

BEN
All right. In a few minutes, okay? Give him a while longer. *(He crosses to the fridge and gets a coke.)*

MARY

I'll get changed then. Keep an eye on the oven, will you? I won't be long. And yell up if he comes in. *(She crosses to the archway, then remembers, crosses back.)* Oh, by the way, how'd it go today? Any luck? You get a job?

BEN

No, I didn't, Mom.

MARY

Oh.

BEN

I didn't look.

MARY

You didn't look? Why not? What was you doing all day?

BEN

I was at the library.

MARY

The library?

BEN

I needed some time to think. I just lost track of time. When I looked out the window, finally, it was dark. So I came home.

MARY

What was you t'inking about?

BEN

Mostly Dad, I guess.

MARY

(as BEN enters the living-room, sits in the arm-chair with his coke) Well, the best way you can help your father is get a job. You can't look tomorrow, but you can start again Wednesday. *(She turns to exit, then turns back to BEN.)* Since when did you start going to the library? You was never that fond of books, even in school.

BEN

Yeah, I know. It happened in Regina last winter. I ran into the library one day to get out of the cold, on my way home from the Post Office. I saw a girl there behind the desk.

MARY

A girl?

BEN

The most beautiful girl I've ever seen. So I picked up a book, any book, just as an excuse to hang around, you know. I did that for weeks, every day except Sunday. I'd go to the library after work and read and look at this girl. Even gave her a name: Sarah.

MARY

Did you talk to her?

BEN

No. I was too shy . . . And one day she wasn't there. I still don't know what happened to her: whether she quit, moved away or got married or what. I kept going back for weeks, hoping to see her again . . . and then one day I realized I was going there just for the books . . . *(He laughs.)*

MARY

(laughing too) Well, just don't tell your father where you was at the whole day. He'd have a fit if he knowed.

She exits upstairs. BEN rises, takes a few paces.

BEN

(exasperated) Shit! *(He paces a moment, then crosses to the window, looks out. Suddenly, he knocks on the window and waves, enters the hall, out of sight. The front door opens.)*

BEN

(off) You want a hand with that, Uncle Wiff?

WIFF

(off) I wouldn't mind, love. Just put it down anywhere.

*BEN enters carrying two fair-sized cardboard boxes. WIFF follows
behind, removes his rubbers. BEN sets the boxes down on a chair in
the hall.*

MARY
(off) Is that you, Jake?

WIFF
No, it's Wiff, Mary. *(to BEN)* Ain't he home yet?

BEN
No. Mom's worried.

WIFF
Yes, well, he's usually home by this time . . .

BEN
She thinks he might've had an accident or something.

WIFF
Well, I wouldn't go that far, duckie. Jake's not the kind to do
somet'ing rash, for all that. He's a good driver.

BEN
Yeah, but he needs glasses. And you saw the mood he was in
this morning.

WIFF
Still and all—Jesus!—it don't help to jump to conclusions. Did
you phone the hospitals?

BEN
No. I didn't want to frighten Mom. I thought I'd phone the
Oakwood first.

WIFF
Now that's an idea. He just might've tied one on.

BEN
(as he enters the kitchen) You know the number?

WIFF
(absently) No, my son . . .

BEN walks to the counter, picks up the telephone book, opens it.

BEN
Uncle Wiff?

WIFF
Yes, my son?

BEN
About this morning . . . Have they been fighting a lot like that, lately?

WIFF
No. No, come to t'ink of it, they've been getting along famously. Like two kids.

BEN
So it's only since I've been home . . .

Sound of truck.

WIFF
Sounds like him, now.

They both look out the kitchen window.

BEN
(crossing to the stairs) Mom, he's home!

MARY
(off) Yes, I heard his truck!

BEN picks up his book and sits on the chesterfield.

WIFF
(as he crosses to the stairs and hangs his coat, hat and scarf on the banister) T'ank Christ. That's a load off my mind. I t'ought

he'd gone off the road and was freezing to death in some ditch. *(He crosses to the chesterfield, sits beside BEN.)* Ben, my son, I just hope we done the right t'ing, persuading him to stay home. I don't mind telling you I've had my doubts, after today.

BEN
So have I, Uncle Wiff.

WIFF
I wish I'd never interfered.

BEN
What if he went in? What do you think would happen?

WIFF
Ben, I wish I had the answer to that one.

BEN
He might be better off, Uncle Wiff.

WIFF
Yes, and who knows? It might be the last t'ing he ever does.

BEN
Well, he'll die if he stays home. At least if he went to work he could keep a little self-respect.

MARY comes quickly down the stairs. She is dressed in slacks, blouse and cardigan. WIFF gets himself a magazine.

MARY
Hello, Wiff. *(to herself, as she rushes into the kitchen)* Better get the supper on the table or he'll have another excuse to be cranky.

She takes the casserole from the oven and is crossing to put it on the table, just as the kitchen door opens and JACOB enters. He shields his left cheek with a rolled-up newspaper.

MARY
(casually) You're just in time, boy. Just this second took the supper out of the oven. You must be famished.

JACOB
(as he crosses to the hall closet and hangs up his coat and cap) No, I ain't a bit hungry. I ate downtown.

BEN and WIFF pretend to be engrossed in their reading.

MARY
I made macaroni and cheese, special.

JACOB
Goddamn it, Mary, why won't you listen to me? I said I wasn't hungry. Don't you understand English? And then you wonders why I loses my temper so much of the time. *(As he crosses and sits in the arm-chair with his newspaper we can see the bruise and cut on his left cheek.)*

WIFF
(casually, from behind his magazine) How'd it go today, Jake? What was you up to?

JACOB
(sitting) Not a goddamn t'ing, Wiff, and I'm the tiredest I've ever been. Doing not'ing takes the good right out of me.

WIFF throws down his magazine and looks at JACOB for the first time.

WIFF
What the hell . . . !

BEN
(looking over) What happened, Dad?

JACOB puts his finger to his lips, indicating MARY.

WIFF
Where'd you get the souvenir, Jake?

JACOB

(smiling) Where else?—the Oakwood.

WIFF

Who'd you run into? Anybody we knows?

JACOB

Only Ike Squires.

WIFF

How is Ike, Jake?

JACOB

Well, a funny t'ing happened, Wiff. Somebody bloodied his nose while I was there.

WIFF

Is that a fact? Sorry I missed it. What hospital's he in?

As MARY enters the living-room and stands behind his arm-chair, JACOB covers his cheek with his hand.

MARY

Is that where you was all day, at the hotel?

JACOB

No, I wasn't. I drove around most of the day and for a short spell I parked in front of the job.

BEN

What for?

JACOB

Don't know. Just to have a look, I suppose.

MARY

What's wrong? You got a toothache?

JACOB

No. What put that in your head?

MARY
What's you trying to hide then?

JACOB
I ain't hiding a blessed t'ing.

MARY
No? Then let me look. *(She pulls away his hand.)* What in the world! . . . Have you been in a fight?

JACOB
(laughing) What makes you t'ink that?

MARY
Stand up and let me look. Stand up. *(He does.)* Stand still. *(He lets her inspect the bruise.)* Better put some Mercurochrome on it. Who hit you? *(She touches his cheekbone.)*

JACOB
(dancing away) Goddamn it, Mary, that stings. Keep your fingers to yourself.

MARY
Who hit you?

JACOB
None of your business.

MARY
Well, I hope it hurts. Who was it, Ike Squires? I heard you say somebody bloodied his nose. You set some example, you do.

JACOB
That's right, Mary, pour on the sympathy. All I did was what you suggested last night.

MARY
What was that, pray tell?

JACOB
(to WIFF) I went after Ike in the beer parlour, instead of the funeral parlour.

Laughing, he exits. BEN and WIFF laugh, too, and so does MARY, in spite of herself.

MARY

Well, come on, you two, supper's ready. *(She crosses toward the archway.)* Jake ain't eating. We might as well start.

WIFF

(rising) No, t'ank you kindly, Mary, I ate before. I just come by to drop some of Dot's t'ings off. *(He crosses to the chair and picks up one of the boxes.)*

MARY

Oh? *(She takes the box.)*

WIFF

(putting on his overcoat) T'ought you might like to look t'rough it and pick out what you likes. The rest you can give to the Salvation Army.

MARY

(crosses to the chesterfield, puts down the box) So you went home after all? I t'ought you'd never set foot in there? *(She sits.)*

WIFF

(crosses to MARY, who slowly removes a beautiful shawl and stares at it) Well, Mary, I left here this morning and went to the cemetery and picked out a plot, two plots, one for each of us, and I stood there with me breath blowing, looking at the white ground and all the headstones round about, and suddenly it went t'rough me like a cold wind: Dot's *dead.* I don't t'ink it had really sunk in before, that fact, even when I bent over her casket last night and kissed her cold lips. Not even then for some reason. Perhaps because she was there in body if not in spirit. Not until that moment in the cemetery did it strike me: Dot's *dead.* Dead. The word itself was like a nail in me own coffin. Tomorrow, I said to myself, she'll be under the snow forever in a bronze box and I'll never see her face again, even in death. In time I'd forget what she even looked like . . . So I had a good cry right there in the cemetery, as

much for myself as for her, I suppose, the first tears I shed since she died . . . And then I got in the car and drove home. Went t'rough the house, top to bottom.

MARY
What for, Wiff?

WIFF
Looking for Dot, maid. Only this time she never appeared. Even sang out her name.

MARY
Wasn't you frightened to, after last night?

WIFF
(sitting) Mary, I suddenly felt that anyt'ing was better than not'ing, maid . . . anyt'ing. I t'ink I understands for the first time a little what Jacob feels . . .

MARY
It ain't the same, Wiff.

WIFF
Ain't it, Mary?

Enter JACOB, carrying a bottle of Mercurochrome and a box of Band-Aids. He crosses to the arm-chair.

JACOB
Here, Mary, put this on for me.

MARY
(*rises, crosses to JACOB*) Did you wash it with hot water?

JACOB
I did. Just stick on the Band-Aid and don't say another word. And don't be rough, it smarts.

MARY
(*as she administers to his cheek*) What'd you do—follow Ike from the job?

JACOB

No, I never. He just happened to be there. Him and a few of the other boys. I sat by myself.

MARY

Yes, for how long?

JACOB

Until I heard them laughing and looking my way. Then I pushed back my chair and went over to his table and asked him to repeat what was so goddamn funny.

WIFF

I'd like to've seen that. That must've shut him up in a hurry.

JACOB

No, Wiff. He t'ought he was safe among his friends. Only a good swift kick in the arse would shut that one up.

MARY

Yes, and you have just the boots to do it. Hold still. *(She pushes him down on the arm of the arm-chair.)*

JACOB

Hold your tongue, Mary. You don't even know what he said to me.

MARY

What?

JACOB

"Sit down, Mercer," he says. "The drinks's on me."

MARY

And for that you bloodied his nose?

JACOB

"You won me five dollars today," he says. "How's that?" says I. "I bet one of the boys five dollars you wouldn't show up." And he gave a great loud horse-laugh. Could've heard him a block away with a band playing.

WIFF
Is that when you struck him, duckie?

JACOB
No, first off I t'rowed his beer in his face, and he lunged up knocking over the table, walloped me one right in the cheek.

WIFF
Sneaky little bugger, ain't he?

JACOB
By Jesus, Wiff, I'll hand him that much, he's fast. Never saw it coming. I only got one good one in before the waiters rushed over and broke it up.

WIFF
Well, next time, duckie, he'll save his bets for the race-track.

MARY
(sticking on the Band-Aid) There. Serve you right if you gets a black eye. That'd teach you.

JACOB
(walking away) Dared me to come into work. Right there in front of the other men. Said I wasn't man enough . . . never had the guts is how he put it. Holy Christ, Wiff, I'd like to make him eat those words.

WIFF
Dare say you would.

JACOB
I'd like to cram every goddamn word down his gullet.

BEN
Why don't you, Dad?

JACOB
What?

BEN
Make him eat his words.

JACOB
How?

BEN
How else? Go in to work.

JACOB
What? . . .

MARY
Ben . . .

BEN
Don't let me stop you. I might as well tell you now as later. I'm going back out west.

JACOB
You is not, now. You just got here.

BEN
I am. I've thought it over.

MARY
Ben, what's come over you?

BEN
Christ, he wants to work, Mom. Let him.

JACOB
Who says I wants to work? I never said a word, did I, Mary? *(slight pause)* Did I, Wiff?

BEN
Come on, Dad, you know you would've gone to work today if we hadn't blackmailed you. You only agreed to keep me home.

JACOB
Listen here, I couldn't care less if I never lifts a bloody hammer again. What's it ever done for me? I'm just a workhorse.

BEN

That's bullshit, and you know it. It's your whole life. *(slight pause)* Anyway, I'm going home . . .

JACOB

Home? . . .

BEN

. . . right after the funeral tomorrow, so you can do what you want. I'm sorry, Mom. *(He enters the kitchen.)*

MARY

(going after BEN) Sorry? You'll be sorry all right.

JACOB

(to himself) I t'ought it was too good to be true . . . *(He sits in the arm-chair.)*

MARY

(to BEN) Have you lost your mind? What do you suppose'll happen now, if he goes in? Have you forgot Ike Squires? He has double the excuse to go after your father now.

BEN

What if he doesn't go in, Mom? Did you ever consider that? Or doesn't that matter?

MARY

He'll never let up on him, Ben. He's that type. You heard Wiff.

JACOB

(explosively) Will you shut up about Ike Squires, Mary? I can snap him in two like a stick of pencil.

BEN

(crosses to JACOB) You'd never let up on yourself, Dad. Or Mom. *(to MARY)* You're the one has to live with him.

WIFF

Ben's right, Jake, as much as I hates to admit it. The boy's right.

JACOB

What? Whose side is you on, Wiff? Mine or his?

WIFF

There's no sides this time, duckie. Don't you know that?

BEN

Look what happened this morning, Mom. That was just the beginning.

JACOB

This morning? What happened this morning? Oh, I see. I ain't allowed to get up on the wrong side, is that it? It's a crime not to have a smile on my face every blessed morning.

BEN

(crosses into the kitchen to MARY) Let him go, Mom. It'll only get worse if you don't.

JACOB

(jumps up, crosses to the hall closet, and gets his coat and cap) All right, Mary. See that, now? He don't give a shit if I lives or dies. He never has. Perhaps you'll believe me now.

BEN

Oh, don't be ridiculous. *(He crosses to the table, sits.)*

JACOB

Well, don't you come to my funeral, you hear? *(to MARY)* And don't you let him within a hundred yards or else. *(to WIFF)* Some friend you turned out to be, taking his part. I never would've believed it, Wiff.

WIFF

Now, duckie . . .

JACOB

Don't duckie me, goddamn it!

He heads for the kitchen door and manages to get just outside, but MARY's next line brings him back.

MARY

(to BEN) Even if what you says is true, Ben, he still ain't fit to work!

BEN

I know that . . .

JACOB

(to Mary) Who ain't fit?

MARY

You ain't, boy. And I'm in no hurry to be a widow, even if Ben's intent on killing you.

JACOB

Goddamn it, Mary, I'll put my fist t'rough that wall if you says I ain't fit one more time. I can still work as good as Wiff here, no odds what you says to the contrary.

MARY

All right, but admit it or not, you're in no condition to be up twenty stories in ten-below cold!

JACOB

Is that a fact? *(He crosses into the living-room, tossing his cap at the foot of the stairs.)*

MARY

(following him) What if you're hanging on with your toolbox and you takes a fit of coughing? Sometimes you can't catch your breath. I've seen it on cold mornings. Even the wind can take your breath away. Or what's worse — what if you has a sudden pain in your chest? What

110

then, boy? Do you t'ink I wants to be sick with worry every day you sets off for the job, not knowing whether you'll be back or not? *(She crosses into the kitchen.)* Ben don't care. He don't have to live with it. *(She crosses to BEN.)* But you'll have to live with it, my son, if anyt'ing should happen to him. It'll be on your conscience for the rest of your life. Is that what you wants? Is it? *(BEN says nothing.)* Well, I just hopes you don't live to regret it, my son. For your sake. I wouldn't want it on my mind, I can tell you. *(She turns and starts wearily for the stairs.)* If anyone wants supper it's on the table. I'm going to lie down. *(She starts up the stairs, then stops.)* He can battle all he wants to, Ben, we're all up against the same enemy: time . . .

She exits. Pause.

WIFF
(rises) Well, I . . . I must be off. *(He crosses into the hall.)* I'd like to be alone with Dot for a spell. May be my last real chance. I won't be back tonight, love. I already told Mary. I'm going home.

JACOB
Oh?

WIFF
Will I see you all later?

JACOB
We'll be there, Wiff, we'll be there. *(then)* Wiff?

WIFF
What, my son?

JACOB
I never meant what I said before. You're the best friend I ever had, outside Mary.

WIFF
Don't you t'ink I knows that, boy. *(slight pause)* And Wednesday morning we'll go to work together. Just like old times. Is that a deal, duckie?

JACOB
That's a deal. I'll pick you up, same time as always.

WIFF
See you later, love. You too, Ben. *(He exits.)*

JACOB removes his coat, hangs it over the banister. Then slowly crosses into the kitchen and gets down a bottle of whiskey from the cupboard. He turns and looks at BEN.

JACOB
You want a drink?

BEN
No, thanks. *(A beat. Then he enters the living-room, sits on the chesterfield.)*

JACOB
(as he pours himself a drink) I never knowed how growed up you was till tonight. *(He crosses to the archway.)* What made you do it?

BEN
Do what?

JACOB
(moves close to BEN) One minute you was willing to stay, the next you wasn't. It wasn't all for me, now, was it? Tell the truth. *(slight pause)* You wouldn't have a girl out west, would you? Is that it? Did I guess right? I did, didn't I?

BEN
. . . Yeah, that's it. How'd you know?

JACOB
(sits in the arm-chair, picks up his newspaper) Well, that puts a different light on t'ings. You ought to've mentioned it before. Now, that I can understand. I missed your mother when I come up here alone to look for work and left her back home. Well, perhaps you'll settle down, at last. What's she like?

BEN
(with difficulty) She's beautiful, Dad. She works in a library.
That's how we met.

JACOB
What's her name?

BEN
Sarah . . .

JACOB
Well, you bring her home next time you comes, you hear? I'd
like to meet her. Will you do that for me?

BEN
Sure, Dad . . . *(He rises.)*

JACOB
(as BEN crosses behind the arm-chair) And don't stay away so
long next time, Ben. *(a beat)* Your mother worries . . .

*He buries himself in his newspaper. Cross fade of lights so that BEN
and JACOB end up in spots, BEN facing the audience. JACOB
remains sitting in the arm-chair, his face hidden by the newspaper.*

BEN
Seven weeks later I took another jet home and stood in a
winter cemetery, stamping my feet against the cold, feeling
somehow he'd set me free with his death. Keeled over on the
job, was how Uncle Wiff put it. Hammering a nail in a joist . . .
      I never did get any closer to my father, though I had
learned to take him seriously as a man, not an obstacle. But
the wall was still there, a little cracked maybe, but still dividing
us, still waiting to be toppled.
      And I never did get to ask him that one simple question
that has haunted me all my life, ever since that summer evening when I was twelve and he came down to the school-yard to
watch me play . . . "How did you like the game?"

*Slowly JACOB lowers and folds his newspaper as though he has
heard the question. The lights fade slowly to black.*

CPSIA information can be obtained at www.ICGtesting.com
Printed in the USA
LVOW11s1211111214

418307LV00010B/19/P